Meat and Poultry

Jeni Wright

First published in 1998 for
Tesco Stores Limited
by Brilliant Books Ltd
84-86 Regent Street
London W1R 6DD

Origination by Colourpath Ltd, London
Printed and bound by Jarrold Book Printing,
Thetford, England

Meat and Poultry

Jeni Wright

About the author

Jeni Wright is the author of more than 20 cookery books, including two on chicken and poultry and several on Italian and oriental cooking. Jeni also writes about food for a wide range of magazines from her home in north London, where she lives with her husband and two children.

Photographer	Laurie Evans
Home economist	Debbie Miller
Stylist	Lesley Richardson
Recipes tested by	Valerie Barrett
	Jacqueline Bellefontaine
	Becky Johnson

CONTENTS

INTRODUCTION

The recipes in this book have been created and photographed specially for Tesco. They have been thoroughly tested and all the ingredients are normally available at larger Tesco stores, when in season. There is no need for any special kitchen equipment.

Using the recipes

1 Both metric and imperial weights and measures are given, except for goods sold in standard size packaging, such as cans. As conversions cannot always be exact, you should follow either the metric or the imperial throughout the recipe where possible.

2 British standard level spoon measurements are used. A tablespoon measure is equivalent to 15ml; a teaspoon measure is equivalent to 5ml.

3 Dishes cooked in the oven should be placed in the centre, unless otherwise stated. Tesco advises that all meat, poultry, fish and eggs should be cooked thoroughly. Poultry juices should run clear when the flesh is pierced with a skewer at its thickest point.

4 Some of the recipes include nuts or nut derivatives. These should not be eaten by children, people who have an allergic reaction to nuts, or women who are either pregnant or breastfeeding. It is advisable to check the labelling of any commercially prepared products to ensure that they do not contain nuts or nut derivatives. Recipes that include honey should not be eaten by children under the age of 12 months.

5 Recipes containing liver or continental meats should not be eaten by children, the elderly, or women who are either pregnant or breastfeeding.

6 Vegetables and fruits are medium-sized, unless otherwise stated. If cooking or serving vegetables or fruits with their skins on, make sure that they are thoroughly rinsed.

7 The fat and calorie content of each recipe is given. These figures are for one serving only.

8 Each recipe has a simplicity rating of 1, 2 or 3 chef hats. Recipes with 1 hat are easy; those with 2 or 3 will require a little more effort.

KEEMA CURRY

Serves 4

Preparation 10 mins

Cooking 40 mins

Calories 274

Fat 14g

Simplicity

1 Heat the oil in a large heavy-based frying pan. Add the onion and ginger and cook over a low heat for 5 minutes or until softened. Add the garlic and minced lamb, breaking the mince into pieces by pressing with the back of a wooden spoon. Cook for 10 minutes or until the lamb browns.

2 Pour off any excess fat from the pan. Add the turmeric, chilli, garam masala and tomato purée, then stir-fry for 1-2 minutes. Add the stock and bring to the boil, stirring, then reduce the heat and simmer, uncovered, for 10 minutes or until slightly reduced.

3 Add the peas, then simmer for 5-10 minutes longer. Remove from the heat, stir in the coriander and season. Garnish with coriander.

1 tbsp vegetable oil
1 onion, finely chopped
2.5cm (1in) piece fresh root ginger, grated
2 cloves garlic, crushed
500g (1lb 2oz) lean minced lamb
2 tsp ground turmeric
1 tsp chilli powder
1 tbsp garam masala
3 tbsp tomato purée
450ml (¾ pint) lamb stock
125g (4oz) frozen petits pois
Salt and black pepper
2 tbsp chopped fresh coriander, plus extra leaves to garnish

This is a really easy way to turn minced lamb into a delicious spicy curry. It's best served the traditional way – with basmati rice, cucumber raita and mango chutney.

GREEK SHISH KEBABS

Simplicity

Serves 4
Preparation 15 mins
plus 4 hrs marinating

Cooking 12 mins
Calories 350
Fat 20g

750g (1lb 11oz) lamb neck fillet, cut into 2.5cm (1in) pieces

Fresh mint to garnish and lemon wedges to serve

For the marinade

100g (3½oz) Greek yogurt

½ small onion, grated

2 cloves garlic, crushed

Juice of ½ lemon

1 tbsp olive oil

3 tbsp chopped fresh mint

Salt and black pepper

1 To make the marinade, mix together the yogurt, onion, garlic, lemon juice, oil, mint and seasoning in a large non-metallic bowl. Add the lamb and stir to coat. Cover with cling film and refrigerate for 4 hours or overnight.

2 Preheat the grill to high. Thread the lamb onto 4 or 8 metal skewers, depending on their size. Grill the kebabs for 10-12 minutes, turning the skewers 2-3 times, until cooked through. Garnish with mint and serve with lemon wedges.

If you've ever been to Greece, these tender kebabs will bring memories flooding back. Serve them with rice, a large Greek salad and some tzatziki on the side.

MEDITERRANEAN ROAST LAMB

Serves 4

Preparation 20 mins

plus 10 mins resting

Cooking 1 hr 30 mins

Calories 610

Fat 27g

Simplicity 🍳 🍳

1 Preheat the oven to 190°C/375°F/Gas Mark 5. Make several incisions in the top of the lamb with a sharp knife and push in two-thirds of the garlic slivers and rosemary. Drizzle with 1 tablespoon of the oil and season.

2 Meanwhile, place the peppers, courgettes and potatoes in a large roasting tin and season. Stir in the remaining garlic, rosemary and oil, then set aside. Put the lamb on a rack in another roasting tin, then roast near the top of the oven for 40 minutes.

3 Place the marinated vegetables in the oven, on a shelf below the lamb, and turn the meat over. Roast for 25 minutes, then add the tomatoes to the vegetables. Roast for a further 10 minutes or until the lamb is cooked. Remove the lamb from the oven, cover with foil and leave to rest for 10 minutes. Cook the vegetables for a further 10 minutes, turning once. Serve the lamb with the vegetables.

½ leg of lamb, about 1.2kg (2lb 10oz)
4 cloves garlic, cut into slivers
Several sprigs of fresh rosemary, cut into pieces
4 tbsp olive oil
Salt and black pepper
3 large peppers (red, green and yellow), deseeded and cut into large pieces
3 large courgettes, cut into large chunks
750g (1lb 11oz) small new potatoes, unpeeled
225g (8oz) cherry tomatoes

...Sunday lunch made deliciously simple. Everything in this dish is cooked in the oven so there's no juggling of saucepans at the last minute. Just relax and enjoy it.

PESTO LAMB WITH CHERRY TOMATO SALSA

Simplicity

Serves 4

Preparation 10 mins

Cooking 10 mins

Calories 484

Fat 33g

12 lamb cutlets

3 tbsp pesto

For the salsa

2 tbsp extra virgin olive oil

2 tsp balsamic vinegar

1 tbsp clear honey

1 tsp Dijon or
wholegrain mustard

225g (8oz) cherry
tomatoes, halved

1 small red onion,
finely chopped

Salt and black pepper

2 tbsp chopped fresh basil, plus
extra leaves to garnish

1 Preheat the grill to medium. Arrange the cutlets on the rack in the grill pan and spread with half the pesto. Grill for 4-5 minutes, then turn the cutlets over, spread with the remaining pesto and grill for a further 4 minutes or until cooked.

2 Meanwhile, make the salsa. Mix together the oil, vinegar, honey and mustard in a bowl. Add the tomatoes and onion and stir until coated in the dressing. Season, then stir in the basil. Serve the cutlets with the salsa, garnished with basil.

Grilled lamb chops coated in pesto are delicious on their own, but the tomato salsa turns them into something special. Serve with new potatoes and a green salad.

SOUTH AFRICAN BOBOTIE

Serves 4

Preparation 10 mins

Cooking 50 mins

Calories 510

Fat 28g

Simplicity

1 Preheat the oven to 180°C/350°F/Gas Mark 4. Heat the oil in a large heavy-based frying pan, add the onion and fry for 5 minutes to soften. Place the bread in a bowl with the milk and leave to soak.

2 Meanwhile, add the minced lamb to the pan and cook for 10 minutes or until browned, breaking it up with a wooden spoon. Add the curry paste, garlic and seasoning and cook for 5 minutes. Add the lemon juice, apricots or raisins and 25g (1oz) of the almonds to the pan and mix well.

3 Lift the bread out of the milk and squeeze gently to remove some of the liquid. Reserve the milk and add the bread to the pan. Transfer the lamb mixture to an ovenproof dish, discarding any excess fat. Whisk the eggs into the remaining milk and season. Pour over the lamb mixture and sprinkle with the remaining almonds. Cook for 30 minutes or until the top has set and is golden.

1 tbsp vegetable oil
1 onion, finely chopped
2 thick slices of white bread, broken into pieces (crusts removed)
300ml (½ pint) full-fat milk
450g (1lb) lean minced lamb
2 tbsp mild or hot curry paste
2 cloves garlic, crushed
Salt and black pepper
Juice of ½ lemon
75g (3oz) ready-to-eat dried apricots, chopped, or raisins
50g (2oz) flaked almonds
2 medium eggs, beaten

This is South Africa's answer to shepherd's pie. Sweet and spicy minced lamb is hidden under a golden topping, scattered with flaked almonds. Serve with a green salad.

LAMB OSSO BUCCO

Simplicity ♟ ♟

Serves 4

Preparation 15 mins

Cooking 2 hrs 15 mins

Calories 385

Fat 18g

2 tbsp plain flour
Salt and black pepper
4 lamb leg shanks, trimmed of excess fat
2 tbsp olive oil
1 onion, finely chopped
1 carrot, finely chopped
1 stick celery, finely chopped
400g can chopped tomatoes with garlic and herbs
1 tbsp sun-dried tomato purée
150ml (¼ pint) dry white wine
450ml (¾ pint) lamb stock

For the garnish

1 tbsp chopped fresh parsley
1 tbsp chopped fresh mint
Finely grated rind of 1 lemon
1 clove garlic, finely chopped

1 Preheat the oven to 160°C/325°F/Gas Mark 3. Mix together the flour, salt and pepper on a plate. Dip the lamb pieces into the mixture to coat well. Heat 1 tablespoon of the oil in a large heavy-based frying pan until hot but not smoking. Add the coated lamb and cook over a medium to high heat for 5-8 minutes, turning frequently, until browned on all sides. Transfer to a deep ovenproof dish.

2 Heat the remaining oil in the pan, add the onion, carrot and celery and cook over a low heat for 4-5 minutes, until softened. Add the tomatoes, tomato purée, wine and stock and bring to the boil, stirring occasionally. Pour over the lamb, cover with foil and bake for 1¾-2 hours, until the meat is tender, turning it over halfway through. Season to taste.

3 To make the garnish, mix together the parsley, mint, lemon rind and garlic. Sprinkle the garnish over the lamb and serve.

The lamb is cooked very slowly in this Italian recipe, leaving it meltingly tender, and there should be enough to satisfy the biggest of appetites. Serve with pasta ribbons.

PORK FILLETS WITH CITRUS AND CIDER SAUCE

Serves 4

Preparation 15 mins

plus 10 mins resting

Cooking 50 mins

Calories 484

Fat 20g

Simplicity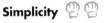

1 Preheat the oven to 190°C/375°F/Gas Mark 5. Put the pork fillets between sheets of cling film and pound with a rolling pin to flatten slightly. Spoon the fruit into the centre of 1 fillet, season and sprinkle with half the spice. Lay the second fillet on top.

2 Stretch the bacon rashers using the back of a knife and place in a line on a board. Put the pork lengthways onto the rashers and wrap them around the meat, crossing on top. Secure with cocktail sticks.

3 Put the pork into a lightly oiled roasting tin and roast for 20 minutes. Turn over and cook for a further 25 minutes or until cooked through. Transfer to a serving plate, cover with foil, then leave to rest for 10 minutes. Remove the cocktail sticks.

4 Meanwhile, pour about 4 tablespoons of the meat juices into a small pan. Sprinkle in the flour and cook, stirring, for 1-2 minutes. Add the cider, fruit juices, honey and remaining spice, then season. Bring to the boil, stirring until thickened. Carve the meat and serve with the sauce and citrus fruit slices.

2 pork fillets, about 300g (11oz) each

8 ready-to-eat dried apricots or prunes, or a mixture of both

Salt and black pepper

½ tsp ground cinnamon or mixed spice

12 rashers streaky bacon, excess fat and rinds removed

Oil for greasing

1 tbsp plain flour

200ml (7fl oz) dry cider

Juice of 1 large orange

Juice of 1 lemon

1 tbsp clear honey

Orange and lemon slices to serve

This is a fabulous, easy-to-carve dish for a Sunday lunch.

Serve with roasted potatoes and green beans.

PAN-FRIED PORK STEAKS WITH ORANGE AND SAGE

Simplicity ♟ ♟

Serves 4

Preparation 10 mins

Cooking 25 mins

Calories 240

Fat 6g

1 tbsp olive oil
Salt and black pepper
12 thin-cut pork loin steaks
300ml (½ pint) chicken stock
Finely grated rind and juice of 1 orange
2 tbsp dry sherry or vermouth
2 tbsp redcurrant jelly
2 tsp chopped fresh sage or 1 tsp dried sage

1 Heat the oil in a large heavy-based frying pan. Season the steaks, add 6 steaks to the pan and fry for 4 minutes on each side or until cooked. Remove from the pan and keep warm while you fry the rest of the steaks. Add to the first batch and keep warm.

2 Add the stock, orange rind and juice, sherry or vermouth and redcurrant jelly to the pan. Cook vigorously over a high heat for 5 minutes, stirring, or until reduced by half and darkened in colour.

3 Stir the sage into the sauce and season to taste. Return the steaks to the pan and heat for 1-2 minutes to warm through. Spoon over the sauce.

Orange cuts through the richness of the pork in this quick and simple dish. Serve on a bed of shredded cabbage with new potatoes and the sauce spooned over.

NASI GORENG

Serves 4

Preparation 15 mins

plus 1 hr cooling

Cooking 30 mins

Calories 439

Fat 13g

Simplicity

1 Cook the rice with the turmeric, according to the packet instructions. Drain, then spread on a large plate. Leave to cool for 1 hour or until completely cold, fluffing up occasionally with a fork.

2 Heat 2 tablespoons of the oil in a wok or heavy-based frying pan. Add half the spring onions, the ginger and chillies and stir-fry over a low heat for 2-3 minutes, until softened. Add the remaining oil, increase the heat to high, then add the pork and garlic and stir-fry for 3 minutes.

3 Add the rice in 3 batches, stirring after each addition to mix well with the other ingredients. Add the soy sauce and prawns and stir-fry for 2-3 minutes, until hot. Transfer to a bowl and mix in the lemon juice. Sprinkle with the remaining spring onions and garnish with coriander.

250g (9oz) long-grain rice

1 tsp ground turmeric

3 tbsp vegetable oil

1 bunch of spring onions, thinly sliced

2.5cm (1in) piece fresh root ginger, finely chopped

1-2 fresh red chillies, deseeded and thinly sliced

225g (8oz) pork fillet, trimmed of any excess fat and thinly sliced

2 cloves garlic, crushed

3 tbsp soy sauce, or to taste

200g (7oz) cooked peeled prawns, defrosted if frozen and thoroughly dried

Juice of ½ lemon

Fresh coriander to garnish

Succulent pork and prawns are combined with rice and aromatic spices to make this simple Indonesian dish. Serve with prawn crackers and plenty of dark soy sauce.

HONEY-ROAST HAM WITH CUMBERLAND SAUCE

Simplicity

Serves 8-10

Preparation 15 mins
plus 3 hrs soaking

Cooking 1 hr 50 mins

Calories 441

Fat 19g

2kg (4lb 8oz) unsmoked gammon joint

1 onion

20 whole cloves

1 tbsp black peppercorns

1 bouquet garni

300ml (½ pint) dry white wine

2 tbsp clear honey

2 tbsp Dijon mustard

For the sauce

4 tbsp redcurrant jelly

Juice of ½ lemon

Juice of 1 orange

75ml (3fl oz) port

1 Place the gammon in a bowl of cold water and leave to soak for 3 hours. Drain, then place in a large saucepan. Stud the onion with a few of the cloves and add to the pan with the peppercorns, bouquet garni and wine. Pour in enough cold water to cover the gammon, bring to the boil, then simmer, partly covered, for 1¼ hours.

2 Preheat the oven to 200°C/400°F/Gas Mark 6. Melt the honey and mustard in a small saucepan. Transfer the gammon to a roasting tin, and cut away the skin and all but a thin layer of fat. Score the remaining fat in a diamond pattern, brush with the honey mixture and stud with the rest of the cloves. Roast for 30 minutes or until the glaze is coloured and the meat is cooked.

3 Meanwhile, bring the redcurrant jelly, lemon and orange juice and port to the boil in a small saucepan, stirring occasionally. Carve the ham into thin slices and serve the sauce separately.

Ham studded with cloves is a great festive dish, especially with this simple Cumberland sauce as an accompaniment. It's wonderful served hot and just as good cold.

CHORIZO AND LENTIL STEW

Serves 4

Preparation 20 mins

Cooking 1 hr 15 mins

Calories 376

Fat 15g

Simplicity

1 Place the lentils in a large saucepan with 1 litre (1¾ pints) water and bring to the boil. Simmer, uncovered, for 20 minutes, stirring occasionally. Meanwhile, place the tomatoes in a bowl and cover with boiling water. Leave for 30 seconds, then peel, remove the seeds and roughly chop the flesh. Drain the lentils and rinse under cold running water.

2 Put the chorizo into a large flameproof casserole dish and place over a low heat until the fat starts to run out. Increase the heat to high and cook, stirring frequently, for 5-8 minutes, until browned.

3 Reduce the heat to low, add the onion and fry for 4 minutes or until softened, then stir in the chopped tomatoes, garlic and chillies. Add the lentils and stock, season and bring to the boil. Cover and simmer for 40 minutes, stirring occasionally, until quite thick but not too dry. Garnish with parsley.

225g (8oz) continental lentils, rinsed

4 tomatoes

225g (8oz) piece of chorizo sausage, skinned and chopped

1 Spanish onion, finely chopped

2 garlic cloves, crushed

½ tsp dried crushed chillies

900ml (1 ½ pints) chicken stock

Salt and black pepper

Chopped fresh flat-leaf parsley to garnish

This spicy sausage stew is typical of Spanish country cooking. It's full of flavour and will satisfy almost anyone's appetite. Serve with crusty bread and a green salad.

BEEF CARBONNADE

Simplicity

Serves 4

Preparation 15 mins

Cooking 2 hrs 30 mins

Calories 506

Fat 20g

2-3 tbsp vegetable oil

1kg (2lb 4oz) braising or stewing steak, cut into 2.5cm (1in) cubes

1 large onion, thinly sliced

1 tbsp plain flour

2 tbsp soft dark or light brown sugar

275ml can stout

500ml (18fl oz) beef stock

1 tbsp tomato purée

1 bouquet garni

Salt and black pepper

Fresh parsley to garnish

1 Preheat the oven to 160°C/325°F/Gas Mark 3. Heat 2 tablespoons of the oil in a flameproof casserole dish. Add a third of the beef and fry over a high heat for 6-7 minutes, turning until browned on all sides. Remove from the pan while you cook the remaining batches, adding more oil if necessary. Set the beef aside.

2 Lower the heat, add the onion and cook for 5 minutes, stirring. Sprinkle in the flour and sugar and stir for 1-2 minutes, then pour in the stout and beef stock and bring to the boil, stirring. Return the beef to the dish and add the tomato purée and bouquet garni. Season and stir well, then cover.

3 Transfer the dish to the oven and cook for 1½-2 hours, until the beef is tender and cooked through. Stir 2-3 times during cooking, adding a little water if necessary. Discard the bouquet garni and season again if necessary. Garnish with parsley.

Almost everyone loves a good old-fashioned stew and you can't beat a beef one. Serve it with plenty of creamy mashed potatoes to soak up the rich gravy.

STEAK AU POIVRE

Serves 4

Preparation 10 mins

Cooking 10 mins

Calories 335

Fat 14g

Simplicity

1 Crush the peppercorns with a pestle and mortar or the end of a rolling pin. Brush the steaks with 1 tablespoon of the oil, then press the peppercorns around the edge of each steak with your fingers.

2 Heat the remaining oil in a large heavy-based frying pan over a medium to high heat. Add the steaks and cook for 5-6 minutes, turning once, until cooked. (The cooking time will vary depending on the thickness of the steaks, so check that they are cooked to your liking before removing from the pan.)

3 Transfer the steaks to serving plates and keep warm. Lower the heat and slowly pour the wine into the pan, then add 100ml (4fl oz) of water. Bring to the boil, then cook for 4 minutes or until reduced by half, stirring constantly. Add salt to taste and spoon the sauce over the steaks to serve.

3 tbsp mixed peppercorns

4 thick fillet steaks, about 160g (5½oz) each

2 tbsp olive oil

400ml (14fl oz) red wine

Salt

Colourful mixed peppercorns give a modern twist to this classic French recipe. Serve with the red wine sauce, French fries or new potatoes and a leafy salad.

ITALIAN MEATBALLS IN TOMATO SAUCE

Simplicity

Serves 4

Preparation 20 mins
plus 5 mins soaking and
30 mins chilling

Cooking 45 mins

Calories 379

Fat 18g

1 thick slice of white bread (crusts removed), broken into pieces

2 tbsp full-fat milk

450g (1lb) lean minced beef

2 cloves garlic, crushed

4 tbsp grated Parmesan, plus extra for sprinkling

1 medium egg, beaten

3 tbsp chopped fresh basil, plus extra leaves to garnish

Salt and black pepper

2 tbsp olive oil

For the sauce

400g can chopped tomatoes with herbs

200ml (7fl oz) red wine, dry white wine or beef stock

2 tbsp sun-dried tomato purée

1 tsp sugar, or to taste

50g (2oz) pitted black olives

1 Place the bread in a large bowl, pour over the milk and leave to soak for 5 minutes. Add the minced beef, garlic, Parmesan, egg, basil and seasoning, then combine well (this is easiest if you use your hands). Roll small amounts of the mixture in your hands to make 20-24 meatballs. Refrigerate for 30 minutes.

2 Heat the oil in a flameproof casserole dish. Fry the meatballs in 2 batches for 5 minutes, turning to brown on all sides. Remove and drain on kitchen towels.

3 To make the sauce, drain the oil from the dish and discard. Add the tomatoes, wine or stock, 300ml (½ pint) of water, tomato purée, sugar and seasoning. Bring to the boil and simmer for 20 minutes, then add the meatballs and simmer for 10 minutes, stirring occasionally. Season to taste, add the olives and heat through for 1 minute. Sprinkle with Parmesan and basil just before serving.

Serve these tasty meatballs, simmered in a rich tomato and olive sauce, with extra Parmesan and plenty of pasta.

BURGUNDY BEEF

Serves 4-6

Preparation 25 mins

Cooking 2 hrs 45 mins

Calories 571

Fat 20g

Simplicity

1 Preheat the oven to 160°C/325°F/Gas Mark 3. Heat the oil in a large flameproof casserole dish until it is hot but not smoking. Add the beef and cook for 4-5 minutes, until it is browned on all sides. Remove and set aside.

2 Pour away any excess fat from the dish, then add the onion, carrot, celery and garlic and fry over a low heat for 4-5 minutes or until lightly browned. Add the stock, wine, brandy, if using, tomatoes, allspice or cloves, bouquet garni and seasoning and bring to the boil. Return the beef to the dish.

3 Cover the dish, then transfer to the oven and cook for 2-2½ hours, until tender and thoroughly cooked, turning the beef over halfway through. Remove the beef, cover and keep warm. Skim off any excess fat from the sauce, then strain into a clean pan, discarding the vegetables. Boil for 5 minutes or until reduced by half. Season and garnish with thyme.

1 tbsp olive oil
1-1.5kg (2lb 4oz-3lb 5oz) boned and rolled beef joint, such as top rump, topside or brisket, trimmed of visible fat
1 onion, finely chopped
1 carrot, finely chopped
2 sticks celery, finely chopped
1 clove garlic, finely chopped
400ml (14fl oz) beef stock
400ml (14fl oz) Burgundy or other red wine
2 tbsp brandy (optional)
4 tomatoes, roughly chopped
Large pinch of ground allspice or ground cloves
1 bouquet garni
Salt and black pepper
Fresh thyme to garnish

A joint of beef becomes beautifully tender when it's been slowly pot-roasted. Serve sliced with some new potatoes and broccoli, and the Burgundy gravy poured over the top.

JAPANESE BEEF WITH HORSERADISH CREAM

Simplicity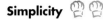

Serves 4

Preparation 10 mins

plus 2 hrs marinating

Cooking 15 mins

Calories 451

Fat 31g

4 rump steaks, about 175g (6oz) each, trimmed of fat

4 tbsp teriyaki or soy sauce

4 tbsp olive oil

6 tbsp crème fraîche

4 tsp creamed horseradish

2 tsp groundnut oil

7 spring onions, finely sliced, plus 1 shredded spring onion

2 cloves garlic, chopped

¼ tsp dried crushed chillies

1 Place the steaks in a non-metallic dish. Pour over the teriyaki or soy sauce and olive oil and turn the steaks to coat. Cover and marinate for 1-2 hours in the fridge. Mix the crème fraîche and horseradish in a small bowl, then cover and refrigerate.

2 Heat a ridged cast-iron grill pan over a medium to high heat. Wipe with the groundnut oil, using a folded piece of kitchen towel. Alternatively, heat the oil in a heavy-based frying pan. Add 2 steaks, reserving the marinade, then cook for 3 minutes on each side or until cooked to your liking. Remove and keep warm. Cook the remaining 2 steaks, then remove and keep warm.

3 Put the sliced spring onions, garlic, chillies and reserved marinade into a small saucepan and heat through. Spoon over the steaks and top with a dollop of the horseradish cream and shredded spring onion. Serve the rest of the horseradish cream separately.

The classic British combination of beef and horseradish is often used in Japanese cooking too. Here it's combined with teriyaki sauce, spring onions and crushed red chillies.

SIZZLING BEEF

Serves 4

Preparation 15 mins

Cooking 20 mins

Calories 328

Fat 14g

Simplicity

1 Put the steak, soy sauce, rice wine or sherry, cornflour and sugar into a non-metallic bowl and mix thoroughly.

2 Heat 1 tablespoon of the oil in a wok or large heavy-based frying pan, add one-third of the beef mixture and stir-fry over a high heat for 2-3 minutes, until browned. Remove and cook the remaining beef in 2 more batches, adding a little more oil if necessary.

3 Heat the remaining oil in the wok, then add the broccoli and 6 tablespoons of water. Stir-fry for 5 minutes, then add the pepper and garlic and stir-fry for a further 2-3 minutes, until the broccoli is tender but still firm to the bite.

4 Stir in the oyster sauce, return the beef to the wok and add the bean sprouts. Toss over a high heat for 2 minutes or until the beef is piping hot and the bean sprouts have softened slightly, then season.

450g (1lb) rump steak, trimmed of any excess fat and cut into thin strips

2 tbsp soy sauce

2 tbsp rice wine or sherry

1½ tbsp cornflour

1 tsp sugar

3 tbsp groundnut oil

150g (5oz) broccoli, cut into bite-sized pieces

1 large red pepper, deseeded and cut into thin strips

2 cloves garlic, crushed

3 tbsp oyster sauce

200g pack fresh bean sprouts

Salt and black pepper

Before you start cooking this colourful stir fry, make sure all your ingredients are cut into pieces of roughly the same shape and size so that they cook evenly.

VENISON WITH CRANBERRY AND RED WINE SAUCE

Simplicity

Serves 4

Preparation 15 mins

plus 4 hrs marinating

Cooking 40 mins

Calories 363

Fat 14g

4 tenderloin venison steaks, about 175g (6oz) each

2 tbsp groundnut oil

Juice of ½ orange and ½ lemon

½ tsp ground allspice

Salt and black pepper

Watercress to garnish

For the sauce

2 tbsp groundnut oil

2 shallots, finely chopped

1 stick celery, finely chopped

1 carrot, finely chopped

250ml (9fl oz) red wine

250ml (9fl oz) beef stock

A few juniper berries

5 tbsp cranberry sauce

1 Put the steaks into a non-metallic dish. Combine the oil, orange and lemon juice, allspice and seasoning and pour over the steaks. Cover and marinate in the fridge for 4 hours, turning twice.

2 To make the sauce, heat the oil in a saucepan, add the shallots, celery and carrot and cook gently, stirring occasionally, for 5 minutes or until lightly browned. Add the wine, stock and berries and bring to the boil, then simmer for 20 minutes or until reduced by about half. Strain into a clean pan, add the cranberry sauce and set aside.

3 Preheat the grill to medium. Place the steaks on a rack and grill for 4-6 minutes on each side, until cooked. Meanwhile, reheat the sauce, stirring occasionally, until the cranberry sauce has melted. Season to taste, then spoon the sauce over the steaks and garnish with watercress.

Richly flavoured venison is just the thing for an autumn or winter dinner party. Serve it on a bed of celeriac and potato mash, with some carrots or a green vegetable.

VENISON CASSEROLE WITH CHILLI BEANS

Serves 4

Preparation 20 mins

Cooking 2 hrs 20 mins

Calories 427

Fat 10g

Simplicity

1 Preheat the oven to 150°C/300°F/Gas Mark 2. Mix together the flour, salt and pepper on a plate. Dip the venison into the mixture to coat. Heat the oil in a large flameproof casserole dish and fry the venison in batches over a medium to high heat for 5 minutes or until browned on all sides. Remove from the pan and set aside.

2 Lower the heat and add the onion to the dish with a little more oil, if necessary. Stir for 5 minutes or until lightly browned, then add the garlic, chillies and chilli powder and stir for 1 minute.

3 Add the tomatoes, beef stock, tomato purée and sugar. Bring to the boil, stirring. Add the venison, stir well and cover tightly with the lid. Transfer the dish to the oven and cook for 2 hours or until the venison is tender, stirring twice and adding the kidney beans for the last 30 minutes of cooking.

2 tbsp plain flour
Salt and black pepper
2 x 340g packs diced shoulder of venison
2 tbsp groundnut oil
1 Spanish onion, finely chopped
2 cloves garlic, crushed
2 fresh green chillies, deseeded and finely chopped
1 tbsp chilli powder
400g can chopped tomatoes
400ml (14fl oz) beef stock
2 tbsp tomato purée
2 tsp soft light or dark brown sugar
400g can red kidney beans, drained and rinsed

Tender chunks of slow-cooked venison are set off by a spicy mixture of beans and tomatoes in this casserole. Serve with rice or crusty bread and a large salad.

STEAK AND KIDNEY PUFFS

Simplicity

Serves 4

Preparation 20 mins

Cooking 2 hrs 45 mins

Calories 650

Fat 35g

4 tbsp groundnut oil
1 onion, finely chopped
500g (1lb 2oz) braising steak, trimmed of excess fat and cubed
350g (12oz) pig's kidney, halved, cores removed, then cut into 1cm (½in) pieces
3 tbsp plain flour
1 tbsp tomato purée
2 tsp Worcestershire sauce
400ml (14fl oz) beef stock
Finely grated rind of 1 lemon
2 tbsp finely chopped fresh parsley, plus extra to garnish
1 tsp dried mixed herbs
Salt and black pepper
150g (5oz) baby button mushrooms
375g pack ready-rolled puff pastry
Fresh rosemary to garnish

1 Preheat the oven to 160°C/325°F/Gas Mark 3. Heat half the oil in a large flameproof casserole dish, add the onion and cook for 5 minutes. Add half the steak and kidney and fry over a high heat, stirring, for 6 minutes or until browned. Keep warm. Fry the remaining meat, adding more oil if necessary.

2 Return all the meat to the dish, add the flour and stir for 2 minutes. Add the tomato purée, Worcestershire sauce, stock, lemon rind, herbs and salt and pepper. Bring to the boil, stirring, then cover.

3 Transfer to the oven. After 1½ hours, stir in the mushrooms and a little water, if needed. Cook for 35 minutes more. Meanwhile, unroll the pastry and cut into 4 x 12cm (4½in) circles. Put on a baking sheet.

4 Take the casserole out of the oven. Increase the oven temperature to 200°C/400°F/Gas Mark 6. Meanwhile, place the casserole over a very low heat. Keep covered but stir occasionally. Bake the pastry for 20 minutes or until golden brown. Top each pastry circle with the steak and kidney. Garnish with herbs.

These puffs have all the flavour of a steak and kidney pie but they're much lighter and very easy to prepare.

LIVER WITH RED GRAPES

Serves 4

Preparation 5 mins

Cooking 20 mins

Calories 321

Fat 18g

Simplicity

1 Mix together the flour, salt and pepper on a plate. Dip the liver into the mixture to coat well. Heat the oil in a large heavy-based frying pan, add half the liver and cook for 2-3 minutes on each side, until cooked through. Remove from the pan and cook the remaining liver, then set aside.

2 Melt the butter in the pan until foaming, then stir in the sugar. Add the vinegar and stir vigorously, then add the stock and bring to the boil.

3 Lower the heat, add the grapes and simmer for 4-5 minutes. Return the liver to the pan and reheat for 1-2 minutes, shaking the pan and spooning the sauce over the liver. Garnish with the parsley.

1-2 tbsp plain flour
Salt and black pepper
450g (1lb) thinly sliced lamb's or calf's liver
2 tbsp groundnut oil
25g (1oz) butter
1 tbsp soft light or dark brown sugar
2 tbsp raspberry or red wine vinegar
250ml (9fl oz) chicken stock
150g (5oz) seedless red or black grapes, halved if large
Fresh flat-leaf parsley to garnish

There's nothing wrong with liver and onions but this French recipe with its caramelised sauce and juicy grapes is in a different league. Serve with herby mashed potatoes.

WARM CHICKEN LIVER SALAD

Simplicity

Serves 4

Preparation 15 mins

Cooking 10 mins

Calories 352

Fat 27g

200g bag mixed salad leaves

2 x 250g packs frozen chicken livers, defrosted

1 tbsp olive oil

15g (½oz) butter

2 tbsp chopped mixed fresh herbs, such as flat-leaf parsley, sage, marjoram or thyme

2 cloves garlic, crushed

Salt and black pepper

For the dressing

6 tbsp olive oil

1 tbsp wine vinegar

Juice of ½ lemon

2 tsp Dijon mustard

2 tsp clear honey

1 Place the salad leaves in a large bowl, then make the dressing. Mix the oil, vinegar, lemon juice, mustard and honey together, then set aside.

2 Cut the chicken livers into large pieces, removing any fibrous bits. Heat the oil and butter in a large heavy-based frying pan. Add the livers, fresh herbs, garlic and seasoning, then cook over a medium to high heat for 5-8 minutes, until browned on all sides. Remove the livers and place on top of the salad.

3 Pour the dressing into the pan, stir vigorously to mix with the pan juices and cook for 3 minutes or until reduced slightly. Pour the dressing over the salad, toss well and serve.

Chicken livers are sensational pan-fried with herbs and garlic, and with a hot vinaigrette drizzled over. Served with crusty rolls, this makes a great supper dish.

CHICKEN ROGAN JOSH

Serves 4

Preparation 15 mins

Cooking 1 hr

Calories 236

Fat 9g

Simplicity

1 Cut each chicken thigh into 4 pieces. Heat the oil in a large heavy-based frying pan and add the peppers, onion, ginger, garlic, spices and a good pinch of salt. Fry over a low heat for 5 minutes or until the peppers and onion have softened.

2 Add the chicken and 2 tablespoons of the yogurt. Increase the heat to medium and cook for 4 minutes or until the yogurt is absorbed. Repeat with the rest of the yogurt.

3 Increase the heat to high, stir in the tomatoes and 200ml (7fl oz) of water and bring to the boil. Reduce the heat, cover, and simmer for 30 minutes or until the chicken is tender, stirring occasionally and adding more water if the sauce becomes too dry.

4 Uncover the pan, increase the heat to high and cook, stirring constantly, for 5 minutes or until the sauce thickens. Garnish with coriander.

8 skinless boneless chicken thighs

1 tbsp vegetable oil

1 small red pepper and 1 small green pepper, deseeded and thinly sliced

1 onion, thinly sliced

5cm (2in) piece of fresh root ginger, finely chopped

2 cloves garlic, crushed

2 tbsp garam masala

1 tsp each paprika, turmeric and chilli powder

4 cardamom pods, crushed

Salt

200g tub Greek yogurt

400g can chopped tomatoes

Fresh coriander to garnish

With its combination of Indian spices and creamy yogurt, rogan josh is a real winner. Serve it with rice, a cooling mint raita and some mango chutney.

CHICKEN WITH SUN-DRIED TOMATO VINAIGRETTE

Simplicity 👨‍🍳

Serves 4

Preparation 10 mins

Cooking 15 mins

Calories 201

Fat 4g

4 skinless boneless chicken breasts
Salt and black pepper
2 tbsp balsamic vinegar
1 tbsp sun-dried tomato purée
175ml (6fl oz) dry white wine or chicken stock
1 tbsp olive oil
Large pinch of sugar

1 Place the chicken breasts between cling film and pound with a rolling pin to flatten slightly. Unwrap and season. Mix together the vinegar and tomato purée in a jug, then add the wine or stock, stirring to mix thoroughly.

2 Heat the oil in a large heavy-based frying pan. Add the chicken to the pan and cook for 5 minutes, turning once, then add the vinaigrette. Cook for 4-5 minutes, basting frequently and turning once more, until the chicken is cooked through.

3 Transfer the chicken to a board and slice diagonally. Cover and keep warm. Add the sugar to the pan juices and boil over a high heat, stirring vigorously, for 3-4 minutes, until reduced by half. Serve the chicken with the vinaigrette spooned over.

Here's an easy way to transform chicken breasts into something extra special, using just a handful of Italian ingredients. Serve with polenta and a leafy green salad.

LEMON CHICKEN STIR FRY

Serves 4

Preparation 10 mins

plus 20 mins marinating

Cooking 10 mins

Calories 290

Fat 12g

Simplicity

1 Place the chicken breasts between cling film and pound with a rolling pin to flatten them slightly. Unwrap and cut into thin diagonal strips. Place in a non-metallic bowl, season, then add the soy sauce, 1 tablespoon of oil and 2 tablespoons of lemon juice. Mix well, cover and place in the fridge for 20 minutes.

2 Heat the remaining oil with the butter in a large heavy-based frying pan until foaming. Add half the chicken strips and fry, stirring, over a high heat for 3 minutes or until golden and cooked through. Transfer to a plate and fry the remaining chicken. Add to the plate and set aside.

3 Mix the cornflour with 1 tablespoon of water until smooth. Add the stock to the pan with the cornflour paste and stir over a high heat for 2 minutes or until smooth and glossy. Stir in the remaining lemon juice and the sugar. Return the chicken to the pan and heat for 1-2 minutes, until piping hot. Serve garnished with the lemon rind and parsley.

4 skinless boneless chicken breasts
Salt and black pepper
1 tbsp light soy sauce
2 tbsp olive oil
Juice of 1½ lemons
25g (1oz) butter
2 tsp cornflour
300ml (½ pint) chicken stock
1 tbsp sugar
Coarsely grated rind of ½ lemon, and fresh flat-leaf parsley to garnish

Chicken breasts are marinated in a piquant mixture of lemon juice and soy sauce, then stir-fried. Serve with a blend of wild and white rice or egg noodles.

CHARGRILLED CHICKEN WITH MANGO SALSA

Simplicity 👨‍🍳

Serves 4

Preparation 20 mins

plus 1 hr marinating

Cooking 20 mins

Calories 237

Fat 7g

4 skinless boneless chicken breasts

1 tbsp olive oil

2 tbsp Thai fish sauce

Juice of ½ lime

Salt and black pepper

Fresh mint to garnish and lime wedges to serve

For the salsa

½ red pepper, deseeded and quartered

1 mango

1 small red chilli, deseeded and finely chopped

1 tbsp olive oil

Juice of ½ lime

1 tbsp each chopped fresh coriander and mint

1 Place the chicken breasts between cling film and pound with a rolling pin to flatten them slightly. Unwrap and place in a non-metallic dish. Combine the oil, fish sauce, lime juice and seasoning and pour over the chicken. Cover and leave to marinate in the fridge for 1 hour.

2 Meanwhile, make the salsa. Preheat the grill to high. Grill the pepper for 10 minutes, cool, then peel off the skin and dice. Peel the mango, cut the flesh away from the stone and chop. Combine the chopped mango, pepper, chilli, oil, lime juice and herbs in a bowl and season. Cover and refrigerate.

3 Heat a ridged cast-iron grill pan over a medium to high heat. Wipe with the marinade, using a folded piece of kitchen towel. Alternatively, heat 1 teaspoon of the marinade in a heavy-based frying pan. Add the chicken and fry for 3-5 minutes on each side, until cooked through (you may have to do this in batches). Serve with the salsa, garnished with mint and lime.

This spicy fresh mango salsa with sizzling hot chicken breasts is outrageously good. Try it with salad leaves, a squeeze of lime juice and new potatoes or rice.

CIRCASSIAN CHICKEN

Serves 4

Preparation 15 mins
plus marinating overnight
and 10 mins standing

Cooking 1 hr 30 mins

Calories 166

Fat 3g

Simplicity

1 Pierce the chicken all over with a sharp knife, then place in a deep non-metallic bowl. Mix together the spices and rub all over the chicken. Combine the yogurt, mint, garlic and salt and spread over the chicken to coat completely. Cover the bowl with cling film and marinate in the fridge overnight.

2 Preheat the oven to 190°C/375°F/Gas Mark 5. Prick the lemon with a skewer and place in the chicken cavity. Place the chicken upside-down on the rack of a roasting tin and pour over the marinade. Add enough hot water to the tin just to cover the base.

3 Roast, uncovered, for 1 hour, turning the chicken every 20 minutes and adding more water to the tin each time. Finally, roast breast-side up for a further 30 minutes until cooked through; the juices should run clear when the thickest part of a thigh is pierced. Loosely cover the chicken with foil and leave to stand for 10 minutes before carving.

1.5kg (3lb 5oz) whole chicken
1 tsp each ground coriander, ginger, turmeric and chilli powder
250g (9oz) natural yogurt
4 tbsp chopped fresh mint
2 cloves garlic, crushed
½ tsp salt
1 lemon

In this Middle Eastern recipe, the whole bird is marinated to give it a hint of spice, mint and lemons. Serve with couscous, roasted vegetables and any pan juices.

CHICKEN AND HAM PUFF PIE

Simplicity 🎩 🎩

Serves 4

Preparation 30 mins

Cooking 30 mins

Calories 710

Fat 34g

1kg (2lb 4oz) whole roast chicken, meat stripped from the bones and cut into cubes

175g (6oz) cooked ham, cubed

98g can sweetcorn with peppers, drained

25g (1oz) butter

3 tbsp plain flour

300ml (½ pint) half-fat milk

300ml (½ pint) chicken stock

1 tbsp Dijon mustard

1 tbsp finely chopped fresh parsley

1 tsp chopped fresh thyme, rosemary or marjoram

Salt and black pepper

1 sheet ready-rolled frozen puff pastry, defrosted

1 medium egg, beaten, to glaze

1 Place the chicken in a bowl with the ham and sweetcorn. Melt the butter in a pan, stir in the flour and stir for 1-2 minutes, until smooth. Gradually add the milk and stock, stirring all the time. Bring to the boil and simmer, stirring, for 2 minutes or until thick and smooth. Add the mustard, herbs and seasoning, then pour over the chicken (add a little extra milk if the mixture is too thick). Set aside.

2 Preheat the oven to 200°C/400°F/Gas Mark 6. Cut out a pastry lid to fit a 1 litre (1¾ pint) pie dish, and a strip to fit around the rim.

3 Stick the strip onto the rim of the dish with water, then spoon in the filling. Place the pastry lid on top, using a pie funnel to lift it above the filling – or make a slit in the centre of the lid. Press the lid down firmly round the edge of the pie to seal. Brush with the egg and cook for 25 minutes or until golden.

Make the most of a few ready-prepared ingredients and you can enjoy the taste of home-baked chicken pie without spending hours in the kitchen.

CHICKEN BREASTS WITH MUSHROOMS AND CREAM

Serves 4

Preparation 20 mins

plus 10 mins cooling

Cooking 45 mins

Calories 350

Fat 21g

Simplicity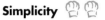

1 Melt half the butter in a frying pan, then add the garlic and chopped mushrooms, reserving the sliced mushrooms. Season and cook, stirring, over a high heat for 5 minutes or until softened. Put into a bowl, stir in the herbs and leave to cool for 10 minutes.

2 Make a slit down the centre of each chicken breast, then insert the tip of a knife into either side of the slit to open it out into a pocket. Place the chicken in a baking dish and spoon the mushroom mixture into the pockets.

3 Preheat the oven to 180°C/350°F/Gas Mark 4. Melt the remaining butter in the pan, add the sliced mushrooms, season and cook over a high heat for 3 minutes. Add the stock, wine and cream, bring to the boil, then simmer for 10 minutes or until thickened slightly. Pour over the chicken, cover with foil and cook for 20-25 minutes, basting halfway through. To serve, spoon the sauce over the chicken and garnish with parsley.

25g (1oz) butter

1 clove garlic, crushed

225g (8oz) chestnut mushrooms, half finely chopped, half sliced

Salt and black pepper

1 tbsp each chopped fresh flat-leaf parsley and tarragon

4 large skinless boneless chicken breasts

150ml (5fl oz) chicken stock

150ml (5fl oz) sparkling or dry white wine

142ml carton whipping cream

Fresh flat-leaf parsley to garnish

A fabulous supper dish that can be prepared a few hours ahead of time and popped in the oven when your guests arrive. Serve with green beans and new potatoes.

POUSSINS PROVENCALS

Simplicity ♟ ♟

Serves 4

Preparation 15 mins

Cooking 55 mins

Calories 542

Fat 36g

4 cloves garlic,
halved lengthways

6 fresh rosemary sprigs,
4 left whole and 2 chopped,
plus extra to garnish

4 oven-ready poussins

4 tbsp olive oil

Salt and black pepper

2 tsp plain flour

300ml (½ pint) chicken stock
or white wine

Juice of ½ lemon

1 tsp Dijon mustard

1 Preheat the oven to 200°C/400°F/Gas Mark 6. Place 2 pieces of garlic and 1 rosemary sprig in the cavity of each poussin, then place them on a rack in a roasting tin.

2 Brush each bird with 1 tablespoon of oil and sprinkle over the chopped rosemary. Season and roast for 50 minutes or until cooked through and tender. Remove from the oven, then loosely cover with foil to keep warm.

3 Remove the rack, then pour the cooking juices into a small saucepan. Stir in the flour, then stir for 1-2 minutes, until smooth. Pour in the stock or wine and bring to the boil, stirring. Add the lemon juice and simmer for 2-3 minutes, stirring, until thickened. Add the mustard, then season. Garnish with rosemary and serve with the gravy.

These tender baby chickens are infused with the flavours of garlic and rosemary. Serve with the lemony gravy, potatoes and some sautéed courgettes.

TURKEY FILLETS WITH PARMA HAM

Serves 4

Preparation 20 mins

Cooking 25 mins

Calories 238

Fat 10g

Simplicity

1 Preheat the oven to 190°C/375°F/Gas Mark 5. Place the turkey fillets between sheets of cling film and pound with a rolling pin to flatten slightly. Unwrap the fillets, cut them in half widthways and season. Heat the oil in a large heavy-based frying pan, then fry the fillets for 2 minutes on each side, until they are seared.

2 Arrange the fillets in a single layer in a baking dish. Place 2 basil leaves on each fillet, then crumple the Parma ham and lay it over the top. Sprinkle over the Parmesan.

3 Add the wine or stock to the frying pan and bring to the boil, stirring, then spoon over the turkey. Cover with foil and cook for 15 minutes. Remove the foil and cook for a further 5 minutes or until the cheese is golden brown.

4 turkey fillets, about 100g (3½oz) each
Salt and black pepper
1 tbsp olive oil
16 fresh basil leaves
70g pack Parma ham
50g (2oz) Parmesan, freshly grated
75ml (3fl oz) dry white wine or chicken stock

If you like Italian food, you'll love this dish. Made with Parma ham, Parmesan and basil, it scores low on effort but high on flavour. Serve with some crusty bread.

TURKEY BREASTS WITH CREAMY MUSTARD SAUCE

Simplicity

Serves 4

Preparation 5 mins

Cooking 35 mins

Calories 456

Fat 28g

600ml (1 pint) chicken stock

200ml (7fl oz) dry white wine

1 sprig fresh tarragon, plus extra to garnish

200ml (7fl oz) double cream

1 tbsp olive oil

Salt and black pepper

4 turkey breast steaks, about 175g (6oz) each, halved lengthways

2 tsp Dijon mustard

1 tsp lemon juice, or to taste

1 Bring the stock and wine to the boil in a saucepan, add the tarragon sprig and simmer for 15 minutes or until the liquid is reduced by half. Add the cream and simmer for 10-15 minutes, until the sauce is reduced by a further third. Discard the tarragon.

2 Meanwhile, heat the oil in a large frying pan, season the turkey and fry for 4-5 minutes on each side, until golden and cooked through.

3 Add the mustard and lemon juice to the sauce, then add the sauce to the turkey. Scrape the bottom of the frying pan with a wooden spatula to mix the pan juices with the sauce. Serve the turkey and sauce garnished with tarragon.

These succulent pan-fried turkey breasts are served in a creamy wine and mustard sauce. If you're worried about calories use half-fat crème fraîche instead of the cream.

TURKEY FAJITAS

Serves 4

Preparation 20 mins

Cooking 15 mins

Calories 445

Fat 25g

Simplicity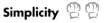

1 Place the turkey in a non-metallic bowl, add the fajita seasoning and mix well. Cover and leave to stand. Meanwhile, place all the salsa ingredients in a bowl and stir in 1 tablespoon of the olive oil.

2 Heat a ridged cast-iron grill pan over a medium to high heat. Dip a folded piece of kitchen towel in the remaining oil and wipe it over the pan. Alternatively, heat the remaining oil in a heavy-based frying pan. Cook half the turkey, turning frequently, for 6 minutes or until golden. Transfer to a serving bowl and keep warm while you cook the remaining turkey, adding more oil to the pan if necessary.

3 Meanwhile, heat the tortillas according to the packet instructions, then pile them onto a serving plate. Spoon the salsa, soured cream and guacamole into separate bowls and serve with the turkey, lime wedges and tortillas.

450g (1lb) turkey stir fry

35g pack fajita seasoning mix

2 tbsp olive oil

8 Mexican flour tortillas

142ml carton soured cream, 120g tub guacamole and lime wedges to serve

For the salsa

2 ripe beefsteak tomatoes, finely chopped

1 small red onion, finely chopped

1 fresh red chilli, deseeded and finely chopped

2 tbsp chopped fresh coriander leaves

Juice of 1 lime

Pinch of sugar

Salt and black pepper

For the perfect fajita, spread a warmed tortilla with guacamole or soured cream – or better still, both – then top with turkey, a squeeze of fresh lime juice and some salsa.

DUCK BREASTS WITH CHILLIES

Simplicity 👨‍🍳 👨‍🍳

Serves 4

Preparation 10 mins
plus 5 mins resting

Cooking 25 mins

Calories 271

Fat 10g

4 boneless duck breasts, about 150g (5oz) each

Juice of 2 large oranges, plus few strips of rind to garnish

1 green chilli, deseeded and finely chopped

90ml (3½fl oz) dry vermouth or sherry

1 tbsp redcurrant jelly

Salt and black pepper

1 Preheat the oven to 220°C/425°F/Gas Mark 7. Score the skin of each duck breast in a diamond pattern. Heat a heavy-based frying pan until hot, then place the breasts, skin-side down, in the pan. Cook over a medium to high heat for 5 minutes or until the skin is browned and crispy.

2 Pour off the hot fat, turn over the duck and cook for 5 minutes. Place the duck, skin-side up, on the rack of a roasting tin and cook in the oven for 10 minutes. Rest in a warm place for 5 minutes.

3 Meanwhile, make the dressing. Place the orange juice, chilli, vermouth or sherry, redcurrant jelly and seasoning in the pan. Boil vigorously, stirring constantly, for 5 minutes or until reduced and glossy.

4 Slice the duck very thinly. Serve with the sauce poured over and garnished with orange rind.

Quickly pan-frying the duck, then roasting it, is a technique that a lot of chefs use to make the meat really succulent. Serve on a bed of bitter salad leaves or rocket.

FRAGRANT DUCK WITH PINEAPPLE

Serves 4

Preparation 20 mins
plus 20 mins marinating

Cooking 10 mins

Calories 203

Fat 9g

Simplicity

1 Place the duck, five-spice powder, soy sauce, rice wine or sherry and sugar in a shallow non-metallic bowl. Cover and marinate for 20 minutes.

2 Heat the oil in a wok. Remove the duck from the marinade and reserve. Stir-fry the duck over a high heat for 2 minutes. Add the pepper, ginger and the white spring onions and stir-fry for a further 3-4 minutes, until the pepper starts to soften.

3 Add the pineapple and juice and the marinade. Stir-fry for 1-2 minutes. Season with salt if necessary. Serve straight away, sprinkled with the green spring onions.

2 boneless Barbary duck breasts, about 175g (6oz) each, skinned and cut into strips

1 tsp five-spice powder

2 tbsp soy sauce

2 tbsp rice wine or dry sherry

1 tsp sugar

1 tbsp groundnut oil

1 orange or red pepper, deseeded and cut into thin strips

5cm (2in) piece fresh root ginger, cut into matchsticks

2 spring onions, white and green parts separated, thinly shredded

175g (6oz) fresh pineapple, cut into bite-sized pieces, plus juice

Salt

Fresh pineapple cuts through the richness of tender duck breasts marinated in Chinese spices. Serve this dish with plain boiled noodles or some fragrant Thai rice.

INDEX